NATURAL MARVELS

Carved by Time

WORLD
BOOK

World Book, Inc.
180 North LaSalle Street, Suite 900
Chicago, Illinois 60601
USA

For information about other World Book
publications, please visit our website at
www.worldbook.com or call 1-800-WORLDBK
(967-5325).

For information about sales to schools and
libraries, please call 1-800-975-3250 (United
States) or 1-800-837-5365 (Canada).

Library of Congress Cataloging-in-Publication Data

Title: Carved by time.
Description: Chicago: World Book, Inc., a Scott Fetzer Company, [2017] |
  Series: Natural marvels | Includes index.
Identifiers: LCCN 2016039088 | ISBN 9780716633655
Subjects: LCSH: Landforms--Juvenile literature. | Uluru/Ayers Rock
  (N.T.)--Juvenile literature. | Antelope Canyon (Coconino County,
  Ariz.)--Juvenile literature. | Cappadocia (Turkey)--Juvenile literature. |
  Danxia Mountains (China)--Juvenile literature.
Classification: LCC GB404 .C37 2016 | DDC 551.3/72--dc23
LC record available at https://lccn.loc.gov/2016039088

STAFF

Writer: Nicholas V. Kilzer

Executive Committee

President
Jim O'Rourke

*Vice President and
Editor in Chief*
Paul A. Kobasa

Vice President, Finance
Donald D. Keller

Vice President, Marketing
Jean Lin

*Vice President,
International Sales*
Maksim Rutenberg

Director, Human Resources
Bev Ecker

Editorial

*Director, Digital and Print
Content Development*
Emily Kline

*Editor, Digital and Print
Content Development*
Kendra Muntz

Manager, Science
Jeff De La Rosa

Editors, Science
William D. Adams
Nicholas V. Kilzer

*Administrative Assistant, Digital
and Print Content Development*
Ethel Matthews

*Manager, Contracts & Compliance
(Rights & Permissions)*
Loranne K. Shields

Manager, Indexing Services
David Pofelski

Graphics and Design

Senior Art Director
Tom Evans

Senior Designer
Don Di Sante

Media Editor
Rosalia Bledsoe

Senior Cartographer
John M. Rejba

Manufacturing/Production

Production/Technology Manager
Anne Fritzinger

Proofreader
Nathalie Strassheim

*Over eons, the forces of nature
have sculpted Earth in certain
locations to create majestic landscapes of great beauty. Some of
the most spectacular landforms
are featured in this series of
books. This image shows Uluru
in Australia from the air.*

This edition:
ISBN: 978-0-7166-3365-5 (hc.)
ISBN: 978-0-7166-3363-1 (set, hc.)

Also available as:
ISBN: 978-0-7166-3374-7
(e-book, EPUB3)

Printed in China by Shenzhen Wing King Tong
Paper Products Co., Ltd., Shenzhen, Guangdong
1st printing March 2017

Table of Contents

Glossary There is a glossary of terms on page 38. Terms defined in the glossary are in type **that looks like this** on their first appearance on any spread (two facing pages). Words that are difficult to say are followed by a pronunciation (*pruh NUHN see AY shuhn*) the first time they are used.

Introduction

Sculpted by wind and water across the ages, landscapes formed through the process of **erosion** (*ih ROH zhuhn*) are among the most beautiful of Earth's natural marvels. Uluru (*OO loo roo*), an enormous rock rising up in the middle of the Australian desert, is one such landform. Sunrise and sunset are especially remarkable, when Uluru appears to glow with a flaming red light. The uniqueness of Uluru has made it a **sacred** destination for **Aboriginal** people of Australia since they first came upon it.

In the United States, Antelope Canyon in the southwestern state of Arizona is another landform created by erosion. The curves and spirals of this sandstone canyon form a serene natural space that has served as a source of inspiration for the Navajo people for generations. At Cappadocia (*kap ah doh KEE ah*), in Turkey, eroded rock formations formed over millions of years create a magical fairyland of towers and spires. Walking along the rainbow landscape at Zhangye Danxia (*Chon yay Dang sha*) in China, shaped by the action of wind and water, feels as if one has stepped into a brilliantly colored painting.

Come explore these natural wonders carved by time. Find out where they are, how they were formed, what makes them so special, and what plants and animals make them their home. Then you can discover why they truly are among nature's marvels.

North America

Arctic Ocean

Asia

Europe

CAPPADOCIA

ZHANGYE DANXIA

ANTELOPE CANYON

Pacific Ocean

Africa

Atlantic Ocean

Equator

Equator

South America

Indian Ocean

Pacific Ocean

Australia

ULURU

Southern Ocean

Antarctica

A landform is a natural feature on Earth's surface, such as a mountain, river, or valley. This series of books, *Natural Marvels,* aims to show some of Earth's most amazing landforms and describe how they formed over time. Some landforms—certain volcanoes, for example—can form rather quickly. But, landforms are usually created over thousands or even millions of years. In these books, you will learn how forces on Earth can, over time, create landscapes of great beauty.

Uluru

Where Is Uluru and What's Special About It?

Revered by **Aboriginal** people of Australia and visitors alike, Uluru is one of the most impressive of Earth's natural monuments carved by time. Also known as Ayers Rock, it is a giant **outcrop** of rock in the Northern Territory of Australia. Aside from its imposing size, the most impressive feature of Uluru is its beautiful range of changing colors throughout the day and across the year. The glowing effect at sunrise and sunset is due to reflective **minerals** in the **sandstone** that change color according to the direction from which the sun's light falls on Uluru.

Uluru is a place of spiritual significance for the local Anangu people. They have looked after the land surrounding Uluru for tens of thousands of years. The Anagu people believe they are **descendants** of ancestral beings who roamed the region in the **Dreamtime,** an ancient time when the world was created.

In 1950, Uluru was officially made into a national park. In 1985, Australia's government returned the land where Uluru stands to the Anangu. In 1993, Ayers Rock National Park was officially renamed Uluru-Kata Tjuta National Park. Kata Tjuta, also known as *The Olgas,* is a group of large rocks 20 miles (32 kilometers) west of Uluru. In 1994, Uluru-Kata Tjuta National Park was made a United Nations World Heritage Site because of its unique environmental and cultural importance.

Uluru, also known as Ayers Rock, rises abruptly from the landscape in the Northern Territory of Australia.

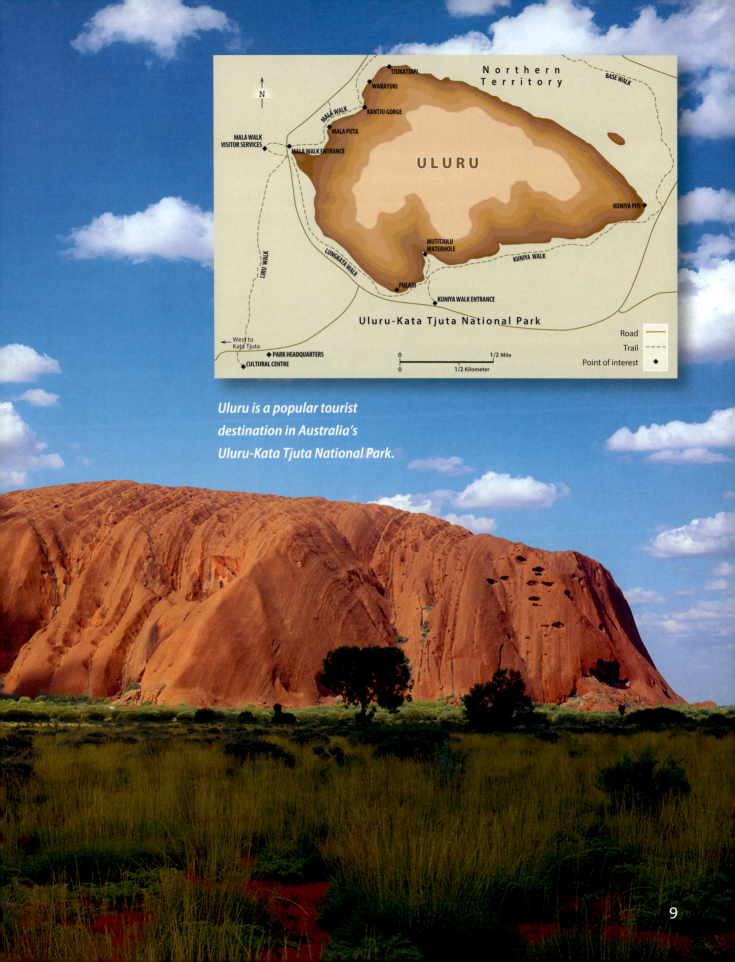

N

TJUKATJAPI

WARAYUKI

Northern
Territory

BASE WALK

MALA WALK

KANTJU GORGE

MALA PUTA

MALA WALK
VISITOR SERVICES

MALA WALK ENTRANCE

ULURU

KUNIYA PITI

MUTITJULU
WATERHOLE

LIRU WALK

LUNGKATA WALK

KUNIYA WALK

PULARI

KUNIYA WALK ENTRANCE

Uluru-Kata Tjuta National Park

West to
Kata Tjuta

PARK HEADQUARTERS

CULTURAL CENTRE

0   1/2 Mile
0   1/2 Kilometer

Road
Trail
Point of interest ◆

Uluru is a popular tourist destination in Australia's Uluru-Kata Tjuta National Park.

Mythical Uluru

The **Aboriginal** people of Australia told this story about how Uluru came to be. A long time ago, at the beginning of time, there lived Alinga (*uh leen guh*), the Lizard Man. He was a powerful warrior. His favorite weapon was his giant **boomerang.** He could throw the boomerang great distances. In fact, Alinga was so big and his boomerang so magical that when Alinga threw the weapon, it would sometimes take weeks or even months to come back.

One day, Alinga decided to throw the boomerang farther than he had ever thrown it before. He launched the boomerang with great force. This time, the boomerang was gone for years. Eventually, Alinga could wait no longer. He set off on a journey to find his beloved weapon. He walked across vast stretches of open desert, but there was no sign of his boomerang. Then one day, Alinga finally found his boomerang.

The boomerang was stuck hard into the ground. So much time had passed and there had been so many sandstorms that the boomerang had turned into a giant red rock. Alinga grabbed the rock and tried to lift it. As he struggled, his fingers carved gulleys and caves in the rock. But the rock was too heavy to be moved. Finally, Alinga gave up and decided to settle down near the boomerang. Today, the Aboriginal people call the massive rock Uluru. All the lizards that live in the caves at the foot of the rock are the **descendants** of Alinga, the Lizard Man.

Aboriginal people of Australia are descended from the first people to inhabit the land. These original people used curved tools called boomerangs (above) for hunting and made elaborate cave paintings (left). The ancestors of today's Aboriginal people arrived in Australia at least 50,000 years ago.

How Was Uluru Formed?

Uluru is known to **geologists** as an **inselberg.** This word means "island mountain." The term describes an isolated rock that rises abruptly from the surrounding lowlands. Uluru is one of the largest inselbergs in the world. It rises abruptly 1,100 feet (335 meters) from the plains, about 280 miles (450 kilometers) southwest of the town of Alice Springs. The rock is more than 1.5 miles (2.4 kilometers) long and 1 mile (1.6 kilometers) wide. It measures 5 miles (8 kilometers) around its base.

Inselbergs often occur in hot and dry regions, where wind and water wear away any **sediments** surrounding the hard rock. Uluru is made up of **sandstone,** the hardened remains of sand laid down on an ancient sea floor. Material continued to collect at the bottom of this ancient sea bed until about 300 million years ago.

Beginning about 500 million years ago, forces in Earth began to lift and tilt the whole area. Eventually, these forces lifted the region to form a mountain range. At the time, there were no plants living on the land, so the rock was bare. Wind and water wore away at the softer rock of this range over millions of years. The **erosion** that formed Uluru probably started about 145 million to 65 million years ago. Eventually, the only part of the mountain range that remained was Uluru. Erosion continues to wear away at Uluru today. Many of the caves at Uluru were formed through the same process.

THE OLGAS

Uluru (left) is not the only rock formation in the region. Kata Tjuta, also called Mount Olga or "The Olgas," is also found in the Northern Territory about 15 miles (25 kilometers) to the west of Uluru. This collection of 36 dome-shaped rocks (below) formed when erosion acted upon a single, massive mountain range over millions of years.

Uluru and Kata Tjuta are two major landmarks within Australia's Uluru-Kata Tjuta National Park.

The Animals and Plants of Uluru

Uluru is in the southern end of the Great Sandy-Tanami Desert in the Northern Territory of Australia. Few plants grow on Uluru itself. The lack of any plants on bare Uluru and the flat sandy plain that surrounds it only add to its stark and mysterious beauty.

At the base of Uluru, however, there are many pools that are fed by rain that runs off the massive rock. Here, lush plant life supports a wide variety of animals. This narrow strip of greenery provided comfortable campsites for **Aboriginal** people when they held ceremonies at Uluru.

The desert around Uluru is home to a wide variety of lizards and snakes. The thorny devil is a common lizard seen here, and many of the snakes are venomous. More than 200 kinds of birds make their home in this desert region or pass through. These include many different parrots, kites, bustards, honeyeaters, and falcons. A plant called porcupine grass provides a thin layer of **vegetation** that covers huge areas of the dry landscape. These plants are important because their roots help hold the sandy soil in place.

Many of Australia's most famous native animals, including kangaroos, wallabies, and wombats, can also be found in the region. Wild dogs, called dingoes, also roam the area.

A lone kite (above) soars above scattered trees (below) that grow near pools around the base of Uluru.

A black-headed monitor lizard (right) and thorny devil (below) search for food on the bare rock of Uluru. The surrounding desert supports only a few hardy plants (below right).

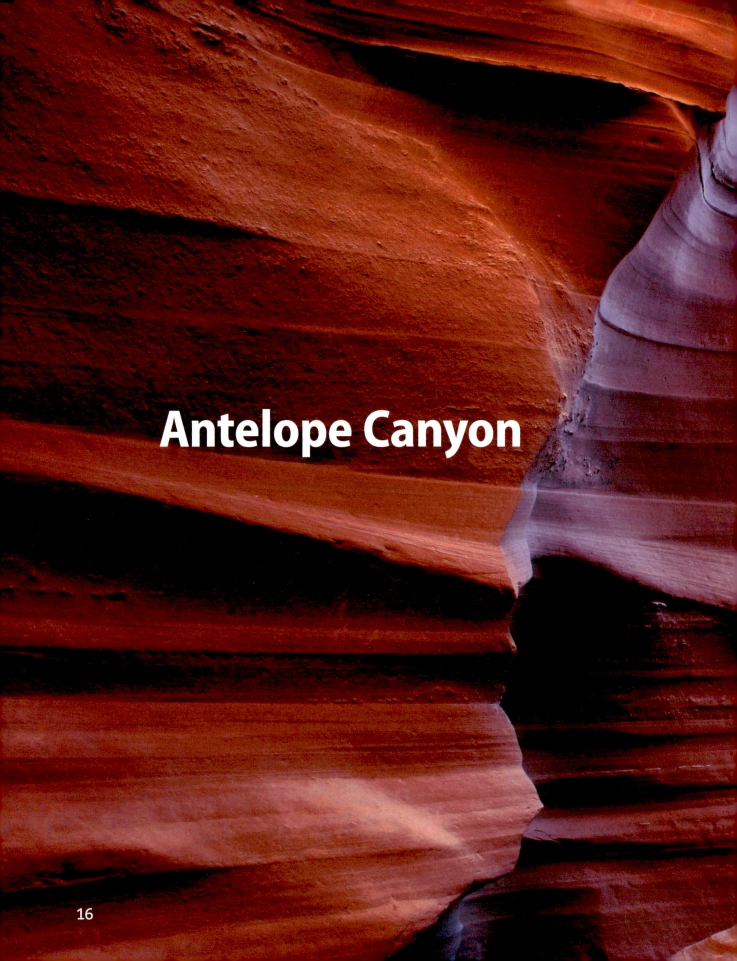

Antelope Canyon

Where Is Antelope Canyon and What's Special About It?

Antelope Canyon is located in the Lake Powell Navajo Tribal Park in the northern region of the state of Arizona in the southwestern United States. It is part of the Navajo nation, a self-governing Native American **reservation.** The Navajo people call Antelope Canyon *Tse' bighanilini,* which means "the place where water runs through rocks." The Navajo call the lower part of Antelope Canyon *Hasdeztwazi,* which means "spiral rock arches."

The narrow passages of Antelope Canyon were carved into the **sandstone** by flowing water over thousands of years. The narrow canyon appears from the outside as a giant **fissure** in the face of a sandstone cliff. Once inside, one immediately feels a quiet reverence. The **pastel** walls, sculpted into arches and spirals, are illuminated by soft sunlight from above. The view constantly changes throughout the day and over the course of the year, as the sun moves across the sky. In some areas, sharp beams of sunlight bounce off the walls to create a dazzling show in an endless variety of shadows and forms.

Navajo people consider the canyon as a **sacred** source of inspiration and harmony with nature. Antelope Canyon is a popular location for photographers, hikers, and sightseers. It is also a valuable source of **tourism** business for the Navajo Nation.

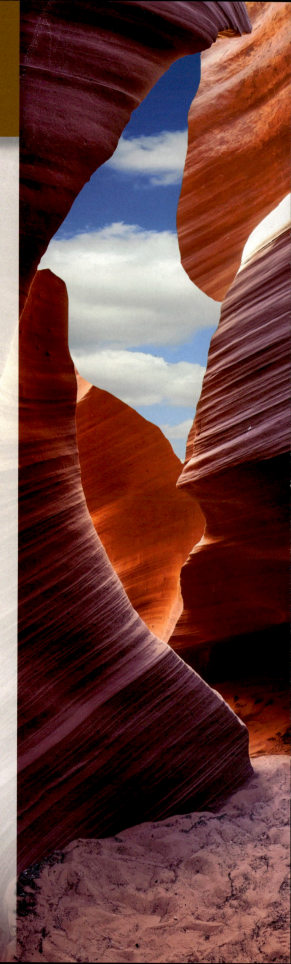

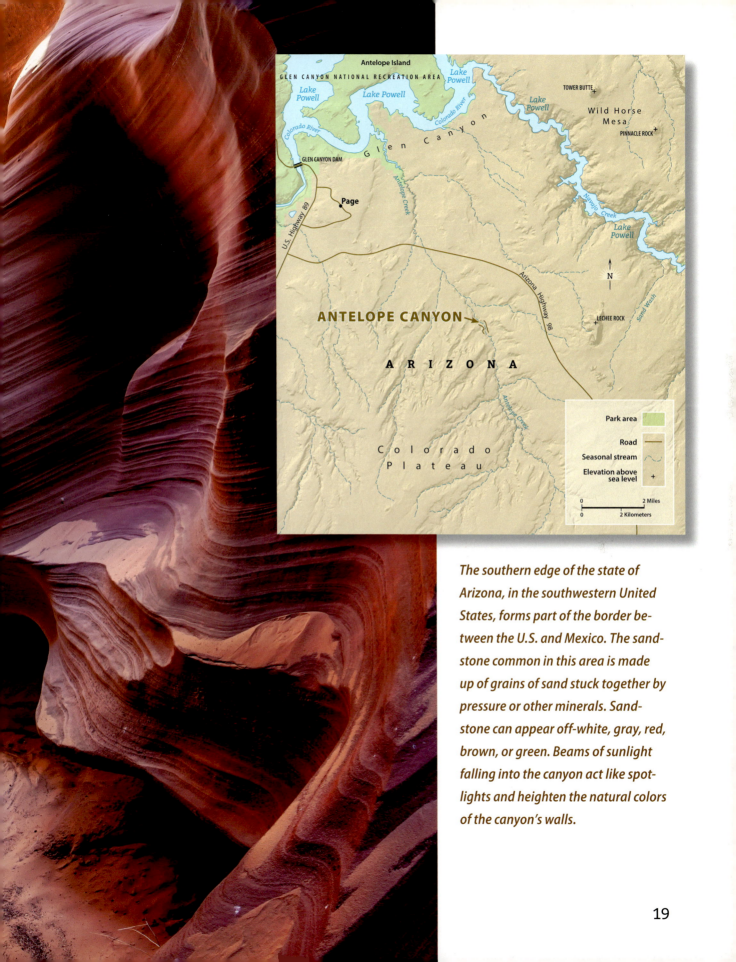

Antelope Island

GLEN CANYON NATIONAL RECREATION AREA

Lake
Powell

Lake Powell

Lake
Powell

Lake
Powell

TOWER BUTTE +

Wild Horse
Mesa

PINNACLE ROCK +

Colorado River

Glen Canyon

Colorado River

Navajo Creek

Lake
Powell

GLEN CANYON DAM

U.S. Highway 89

Page

Antelope Creek

N

Arizona Highway 98

Sand Wash

LECHEE ROCK +

ANTELOPE CANYON →

A R I Z O N A

C o l o r a d o
P l a t e a u

Antelope Creek

Park area

Road

Seasonal stream

Elevation above
sea level +

0   2 Miles
0   2 Kilometers

The southern edge of the state of
Arizona, in the southwestern United
States, forms part of the border between the U.S. and Mexico. The sandstone common in this area is made
up of grains of sand stuck together by
pressure or other minerals. Sandstone can appear off-white, gray, red,
brown, or green. Beams of sunlight
falling into the canyon act like spot-
lights and heighten the natural colors
of the canyon's walls.

19

How Was Antelope Canyon Formed?

Geologists call Antelope Canyon a "slot canyon." These deep **crevices** are always much deeper than they are wide. Antelope Canyon's walls range from 3 to 10 feet (1 to 3 meters) wide and up to 165 feet (50 meters) deep.

A slot canyon may start out as a dry creek bed, **gulch,** or even a small crack in a rock surface. It does not rain often in the Arizona desert, but seasonal rains can be heavy. The hard, dry desert cannot soak up the rainwater, which flows rapidly down the path of least resistance. Rushing water wears away the soft sandstone, making a shallow gulch or crack bigger and deeper. Rocks and pebbles are loosened and washed away as the crack widens. Later, rushing waters flowing through the widened **fissure** create pressure that helps the water blast away more rock like a fire hose. The tumbling rocks themselves smash through the sandstone, opening a wider channel. Finally, a narrow, deep canyon is formed. The canyon walls bend, ripple, and spiral, in complex patterns sculpted by rushing water.

But this beauty can hide real danger. Hikers passing through Antelope Canyon must beware of flash floods that can strike without warning. Torrents of water can come crashing into the narrow canyon from rains that fell miles away. By the time a hiker inside the canyon hears the thunderous roar of the water it may already be too late to find safety.

Seen from above, Antelope Canyon (left) looks like a jagged crack in the earth. But inside, the walls are smooth and curved (above).

21

The Animals and Plants of Antelope Canyon

Herds of pronghorn antelope once roamed freely around Antelope Canyon. They are not so common in the region today. The pronghorn looks like an antelope, but it is actually not closely related to antelope or to any other animal with horns or hoofs. Pronghorns have black horns with backward curved tips. A hooklike prong sticks out from the front and middle of each horn. The pronghorn ranks as the fastest **mammal** in the Western Hemisphere. It runs at speeds up to 60 miles (96 kilometers) per hour.

Life is spread thinly across the desert landscape, but many animals and plants make their home around the canyon. Among them are mule deer and white-tailed deer, elk, and bighorn sheep. Other animals that may be seen include foxes, raccoons, skunks, and squirrels. Arizona is also home to the collared peccary or *javelina,* an animal distantly related to the wild hog. Birds in the region include doves, grouse, and quail.

Arizona has over 40 kinds of lizards, including the poisonous Gila monster. Rattlesnakes live in most parts of the state, and the poisonous coral snake is found in the desert. Scorpions and tarantulas are also common in the desert.

Arizona is famous for its cactuses. The sharp-spined cholla cactus is common in the hot desert areas. Creosote bushes are also common. Wildflowers include the golden columbine, paintbrush, poppy, and sand verbena.

Few pronghorn antelope (above) roam near Antelope Canyon today, while the house finch (right) and the Gila monster (below) are more common sights.

A collared peccary, or javalina (right), forages among cactus in the Arizona desert. The common cholla cactus (below right) blooms from April through June.

Cappadocia

Where Is Cappadocia and What's Special About It?

Cappadocia (*kap ah doh KEE ah*), on the high plains of central Turkey, is an extraordinary marvel of nature steeped in the history of many empires. In Turkish, Cappadocia is called *Kapadokya,* meaning "Land of Beautiful Horses." Many tourists visit the region each year to see its natural wonders.

Cappadocia is famous for its spectacular natural rock **formations.** White rocks in the shapes of giant columns, cones, mushrooms, ridges, and towers called "fairy chimneys" dot the land. Folktales claim that fairies living underground came up to the surface through the towers. Some of the formations reach more than 130 feet (40 meters) into the sky. Other areas feature bright white ridges that glow red and gold at sunrise and sunset.

Over time, people added to the unusual landscape at Cappadocia by burrowing into the soft rock. They created caves, churches, homes, and even entire towns within the rocks. Cappadocia's most spectacular rock dwellings are in the Göreme (*GURR eh meh*) Valley. There, a network of caves, complexes, and tunnels includes churches and convents dating from the A.D. 300's. Göreme National Park and the Rock Sites of Cappadocia were named a World Heritage Site in 1985. Such sites are places of unique cultural or natural importance as designated by UNESCO, the United Nations Educational, Scientific and Cultural Organization.

The spectacular formations of Cappadocia (left) are composed of soft rock, easily carved into homes and churches (below).

27

How Was Cappadocia Formed?

Millions of years ago, volcanic eruptions covered Cappadocia in thick layers of chalky ash capped by a layer of harder rock called **basalt.** Over centuries the volcanic ash solidified into a spongy rock called **tuff.** Wind, rain, snow, and rivers caused **erosion** that acted upon the bedrock to form the unusual rock **formations** at Cappadocia.

The climate in the region, with hot summers and cold winters, heavy rains, and melting snow in the spring, played an important role in making the landscape at Cappadocia. Heavy rainfall eroded the flat land into a network of deep gullies and **fissures** in the rock. Sometimes, raging rivers wore quickly through the soft rock, leaving steep-sided triangular peaks.

Cappadocia's distinctive "fairy chimneys" were formed when hard basalt covered thick layers of tuff. In some spots, the basalt cracked and fell away. Rain and wind wore away at the softer tuff. In some spots, however, the basalt remained like a cap, protecting the tuff. Over time, only an isolated pinnacle of soft rock with a basalt cap remained.

The action of wind, rain, and snow over thousands of years carved the unusual rock formations (right) found at Cappadocia.

AN UNDERGROUND CITY

At Derinkuyu (*DUR in KOO yu*), the deepest of the underground cities at Cappadocia, the massive carved space consists of eight separate floors. The site includes homes, churches, livestock stalls (above), wine cellars, and schools. Miles of tunnels, used in times of war, crisscross the underground city. They provided shelter and defense from invading armies. Historians believe it was built more than 1,000 years ago. But it was not discovered until 1963.

Cappadocia Over Time

The magical landforms at Cappadocia were carved by nature and people over many years. The soft rock that makes up the land was created by the action of volcanoes long ago. The action of wind and water produced some of the landforms that are found there today. When people arrived in the region thousands of years ago, they found the soft rock perfect for making homes.

SUBTERRANEAN CITIES

Over many years, people carved houses, shops, and even churches into the soft rock of Cappadocia. Some of these underground cities (left) extend many levels beneath the surface.

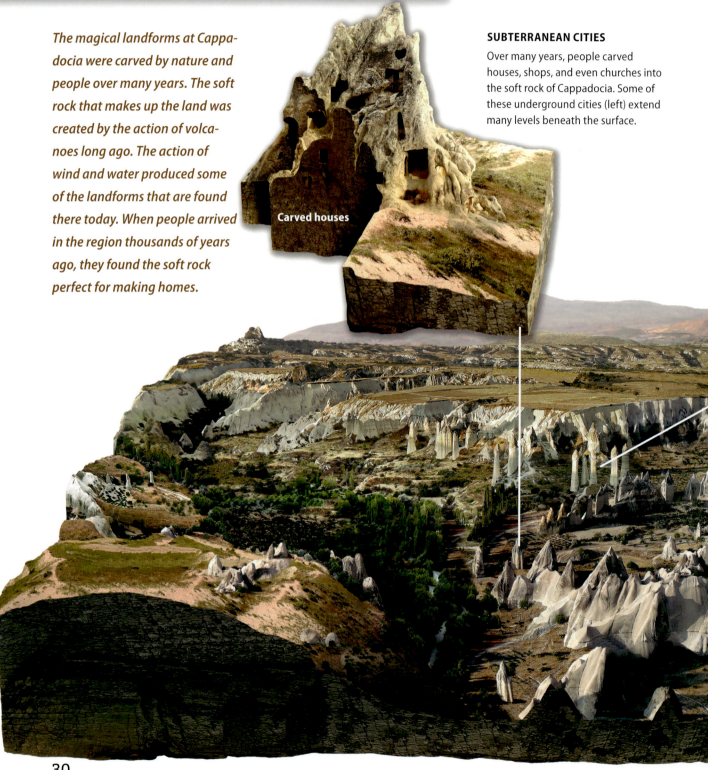

Carved houses

BEWITCHING LANDSCAPES

The distinctive "fairy chimneys" at Cappadocia (below) are made up of a "body" and "neck" of soft rock with a cap of hard basalt rock at the top.

Cap

Neck

Body

Fairy chimneys can reach heights of 130 feet (40 meters).

HOW CHIMNEYS WERE FORMED

Cappadocia's "fairy chimneys" were formed by the eruption of nearby volcanoes and the action of wind and water over thousands of years.

1. Nearby volcanoes erupted millions of years ago, depositing ash over the land.

2. Over time, the ash solidified into a soft rock called tuff.

3. Later eruptions deposited a layer of hard basalt over the tuff. Wind and water began to wear away both kinds of rock.

4. In some areas, columns of tuff, capped by basalt, resisted erosion and were left standing as "chimneys."

Zhangye Danxia

How Was Zhangye Danxia Formed?

Walking among the colored rocks at Zhangye Danxia (*Chon yay Dang sha*) in Gansu Province, north-central China, you may feel as if you are stepping into a painting. The region is famous for its magnificent multicolored **sandstone** hills that stretch to the horizon. The colorful stripes of sandstone here seem too bright and deeply hued to be real. The colors are even more vibrant after it rains.

The Danxia landscapes of China were formed more than 100 million years ago. Layers of sand were laid down over millions of years in an ancient sea bed. Time and pressure from the built- up **sediments** turned these layers into sandstone. More than 6 million years ago, the layers of sandstone were folded and uplifted by forces deep within Earth.

Zhangye Danxia may contain the greatest variety of natural stone colors in the world. The red color is caused by an iron-rich **mineral** called hematite (*HEHM uh tyt*) in the sandstone. The yellow colors are due to the presence of sand and smaller **sediments** that make up clay in the layers. Blue, green, and gray colors in some layers are caused by the presence of a mineral called glauconite (*GLAW kuh nyt*) that forms in ocean sediments.

The mineral hematite creates the red color in the rock of Zhangye Danxia. Hematite is a mixture of iron and oxygen. The word hematite means "like blood." Combinations of sand and other minerals create different colors at Zhangye Danxia.

Zhangye Danxia Throughout History

Zhangye Danxia is part of the northern route of the famous Silk Road. The Silk Road was a group of ancient trade routes that connected China and Europe. The Silk Road flourished mainly from the 100's B.C. to the A.D. 1500's. The routes stretched across about 5,000 miles (8,000 kilometers). They crossed mountains and deserts in central Asia and the Middle East between eastern China and the Mediterranean Sea. The Silk Road got its name from the vast amount of Chinese silk carried along it for trade.

Many cities and towns along the Silk Road provided food, water, and rest for travelers. They also offered goods for trade. Today, those towns serve tourists visiting Zhangye Danxia.

Caravans carried most goods across desert regions along the Silk Road using two-humped Bactrian camels. These sturdy animals, whose ancestors roamed wild in the region, can carry heavy packs for long distances over rocky mountain trails. Perhaps a few hundred wild Bactrian camels still survive in Mongolia, and over a million are still used for transport in Asia.

By A.D. 800, traffic began to decrease as traders started to travel by safer sea routes. A final period of heavy use occurred during the 1200's and 1300's, when a people known as the Mongols ruled central Asia and China. Today, the Zhangye Danxia is protected as a National Park.

A European map from the year 1375 (below) depicts merchants carrying goods along the Silk Road, an ancient trade route that passed through Zhangy Danxia (left) connecting Europe and China.

Glossary

Aboriginal the first or earliest people to live in a particular region

basalt a hard, dark-colored volcanic rock

boomerang a curved piece of wood used as a weapon by Aboriginal people of Australia

crevice a narrow split or crack

descendant an offspring; child, great-grandchild, and so on. You are a direct descendant of your parents, grandparents, great-grandparents, and earlier ancestors

Dreamtime a fundamental spiritual concept that connects traditional beliefs and practices among the Aboriginal people of Australia. Dreamtime includes an ancient time when the first beings existed. It is also a timeless feature of the universe

erosion the natural process of wearing away by glaciers, temperature changes, running water, waves, ice, or wind

fissure a long, narrow opening, split, or crack

formation a series of layers or deposits of the same kind of rock or mineral

geologist a scientist who studies rocks, soils, mountains, volcanoes, rivers, oceans, and other parts of Earth

gulch a very deep, narrow ravine with steep sides, especially one marking the course of a stream

inselberg a core of a mountain left rising above a surrounding plain primarily by the process of wind erosion

mammal a warm-blooded animal that feeds its young on the mother's milk

mineral any substance neither plant nor animal. Salt and sand are minerals

outcrop rock exposed at Earth's surface

pastel a soft, pale shade of a color

reservation an area of United States land set aside, or reserved, for American Indians as a permanent tribal homeland

sacred having religious importance

sandstone a kind of rock formed mostly of sand, the grains being held together by a natural cement

sediment grains of earth, stones, or other matter suspended in or deposited by water, wind, or ice

tourism the act or practice of touring or traveling for pleasure or the business of serving tourists

tuff a soft rock produced by the compression of volcanic ash and other volcanic fragments

vegetation plant life

Find Out More

Erosion: Changing Earth's Surface by Robin Koontz (Picture Window Books, 2007) *Learn more about the natural effects of erosion in this colorful book.*

Cracking Up: A Story About Erosion by Jacqui Bailey and Matthew Lilly (Picture Window Books, 2006) *Understand how weather and water wear away rocks to create new formations.*

Erosion by Shirley Smith Duke (Rourke Educational Media, 2015) *Understand the effects of erosion on our planet.*

Use Your Noodle!

All of the landforms seen in this book were formed by the action of erosion on rocks. How do you think the type of rock affects the way it erodes? What qualities do you think make certain rocks more likely to be changed by erosion than other rocks? Can you find any examples of erosion in the area where you live?

Acknowledgments

Cover © Stock Connection/SuperStock
4-5 © Shutterstock
6-7 © Stock Connection/SuperStock
8-9 © Simon Bradfield, iStock
10-11 © Marc Witte, Shutterstock; © Stock Connection/SuperStock
12-13 © Thierry Grun, age fotostock/SuperStock; © age fotostock/SuperStock
14-15 © Peter Zurek, Shutterstock; © John Carnemolla, Shutterstock; © Jean-Paul Ferrero, Ardea.com/Pantheon/SuperStock; © iStock; © Kris Nootenboom, Shutterstock; © Simon Bradfield, iStock
16-19 © Shutterstock
20-21 © age fotostock/Alamy Images; WORLD BOOK photo by Tom Evans
22-23 © Shutterstock; © George Grall, Exactostock-1701/SuperStock; © Shutterstock; © Martha Marks, Shutterstock; © Christopher Gardiner, Shutterstock; © Anton Foltin, Shutterstock
24-25 © iStock
26-27 © Filip Fuxa, Shutterstock
27 © iStock
28-29 © iStock; © REDA & CO srl/Alamy Images
30-31 © Sol 90 Images
32-33 © Shutterstock
34-35 © iStock; © Sabena Jane Blackbird, Alamy Images
36-37 © Shutterstock; © M.C.Esteban, Iberfoto/Mary Evans Picture Library

Index